ECO-HEROES, Agents of Change

My sincere thanks to the following people for their time, information, images and enthusiasm for this book:

Beryl Kay, Shimon Schwarzschild and the team at Action for Nature, San Francisco, USA

Alexander Zerphy and his family, Maryland, USA

Roz Savage, London, UK

June Barnard, Perth, Australia

Australia Post, Melbourne, Australia

Brendan Condon, Melbourne, Australia

Dear Reader

Every day, we hear about unsustainable practices around the world. Fortunately, there are many eco-heroes who are passionate about reversing the adverse effects of environmentally harmful practices.

Who do you think are the best eco-heroes on Earth? In my opinion, they are the plants and animals that have co-existed in their natural habitats for millions of years. But people can be amazing eco-heroes, too.

INSPIRATIONAL KIDS WIN INTERNATIONAL ECO-HERO AWARDS – SEE CHAPTER 3.

One of my favourite eco-heroes is Roz Savage, who is rowing solo around the world to bring attention to the serious problem of widespread plastic pollution in our oceans. She started in 2005, and Roz is still rowing today!

I hope you enjoy reading about Roz and the other eco-heroes featured in this book.

Sharon Parsons

Contents

ECO-HEROES, Agents of Change

1 Everyone Can Be an Eco-Hero

The toco toucan is the largest in the toucan family and is found in parts of central and eastern South America.

Nature at its Best

The best eco-heroes on our planet are the many species of plants and non-human animals that have lived on Earth for millions of years. In their natural habitats, these plants and animals live sustainably, in a balance with the other living things around them.

For a long time, humans coexisted with nature in sustainable ways. But as people around the world invented more and more advanced technologies, environmental problems appeared. Some of these are:

a white-faced capuchin in the Costa Rican rainforest

1. widespread pollution in the environment and atmosphere
2. the increase of mass consumerism, leading to increased waste
3. more extinct, endangered and threatened species

Recycle More Re-Use More

Eco-Heroes Worldwide

In recent decades, millions of eco-heroes have emerged around the world. These are people working to prevent further environmental deterioration. Environmentalists campaign in all kinds of ways to protect the air, water, soil and ecosystems. Despite all the good work being done for our environment, we can do more.

The most important message is that everyone can be an eco-hero. It does not matter how small your actions are, every eco-action adds up to one big positive impact on Earth.

compost bins

What Eco-Actions Can You Do Today?
Save Water When You Brush Your Teeth
Tap Off for First Brush
E
Tap On to Rinse Brush
Tap Off for Second Brush
E
Tap On for Final Rinse
E

Recycle for Rabbits

Give Leftover Leafy Vegetables and Phone Books to Your Pet Rabbits

Health

The RSPCA's Guide to a Healthy Rabbit Diet

The Royal Society for the Prevention of Cruelty to Animals (RSPCA) suggests: two packed cups of leafy green vegetables such as broccoli, cabbage, carrot tops, parsley or spinach + one or two tablespoons of treats, such as fruits and carrots + plenty of fresh water + old phone books to chew on. Avoid: grains, nuts, seeds, corn, beans, peas, bread, biscuits, sugar and chocolate.

2 Earth Day – One Billion Eco-Heroes

On 22 April 1970 the first Earth Day was launched in the USA. That year, about 20 million people discussed pollution affecting Earth's atmosphere, land, oceans and waterways. Earth Day discussions inspired the United States government to:

- pass clean air and water laws
- pass laws about protecting endangered species
- establish the Environmental Protection Agency (EPA). The EPA's role is to research, investigate environmental issues and enforce environmental laws.

Earth Day in Florida – Soldiers Pick Up Trash

Earth Day in Texas – Clothes Made From Trash

On Earth Day 2011, soldiers picked up trash at a Naval Air Station in Florida, USA.

Eco-fashion girls model clothes made from trash for the TRASHIONISTA eco-fashion show at an Earth Day Festival in Texas, USA.

Earth Day Inspires Positive Actions

Every year, Earth Day is celebrated on 22 April. About one billion people in over 170 countries participate in all kinds of eco-actions in homes, schools and communities. Earth Day reminds everyone, including governments, that it is important to continue caring for planet Earth and all living things.

ECO-ACTION

An "eco-action" is any action or activity that makes a positive contribution to the work of protecting and caring for our environment.

Thai Buddhist Monks in prayer at the Dhammakaya Temple north of Bangkok, Thailand.

Thousands in Thailand

Thai monks were joined by around 200 000 visitors who all dressed in white for Earth Day 2009.

The celebration was also to mark the completion of a temple decorated with one million small bronze Buddha statues!

A crowd spells out "CO_2" with a down arrow on Earth Day 2010 in Taipei, Taiwan.

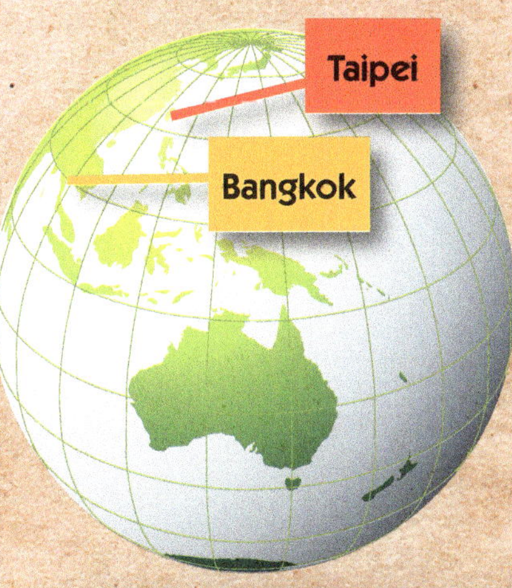

Earth Day Canada

Earth Day Canada is an organisation based in the city of Toronto. Every year their work inspires about six million Canadians to participate in Earth Day activities. Throughout the year, Earth Day Canada also organises many activities, such as earth walks, festivals and clean-up campaigns.

EARTH DAY LAUNCHED INTERNATIONALLY

In 1990, Earth Day was officially launched in about 140 countries and about 200 million people participated in many activities.

Toronto

Earth Day in Washington, DC, USA

Washington, DC

A model of Earth was covered with plastic trash bags at a rally for climate change at the mall in Washington, DC, for Earth Day 2010.

ENVIRONMENT FEATURE

Eco-Hero Organisations

In recent years, an increasing number of organisations have been established to inspire kids to become eco-heroes, too. These organisations are run by dedicated people who donate their time and resources so they can help to preserve Earth for future generations.

Action for Nature is an eco-hero organisation based in Assisi, Italy, and San Francisco, USA. Action for Nature encourages young people to **act for nature**. Read more about their awards for kids in Chapter 3.

Eco-Hero Helps Songbirds

Shimon Schwarzschild is the founder of Action for Nature. He began his career as an eco-hero on a visit to Assisi in Italy in 1982. He discovered that Assisi songbirds were being hunted, killed and eaten. He started a campaign to protest the hunting of the birds. Many people helped his campaign and in 1984 the city of Assisi banned the hunting of songbirds. Shimon then founded Action for Nature, to encourage other people, especially kids, to take action to protect our natural environment.

Assisi

Shimon Schwarzschild with a dolphin, at Monkey Mia, Western Australia

3 Eco-Hero Kids

Every year, Action for Nature invites children from around the world to enter the International Eco-Hero Awards. There are two age groups: 8–13 and 14–16. Beryl Kay, president of Action for Nature, is proud of the hundreds of children who donate their time to worthy environmental causes every year.

Beryl Kay, President of Action for Nature

Adarsha Shivakumar (15 years old) and Apoorva Rangan (14 years old) earned first place in 2009 for starting a Jatropha biofuel project in India.

Samantha Muscarella (ten years old) earned an honourable mention in 2009 for her clean-up and recycling programs in New York, USA.

Brandon Wood (nine years old) earned an honourable mention in 2010 for raising funds to support a chimpanzee sanctuary in the USA.

ECO-KIDS 4 ECOSYSTEMS

Liam Bane O'Neil (11 years old) earned second place in 2010 for starting a community garden project in his town in the USA.

Adeline Suwana (12 years old) earned first place in 2009 for starting a variety of environmental projects in Indonesia.

Alexander Zerphy, Eco-Hero

In 2010, Alexander Zerphy became an official eco-hero! Alexander won first place in the International Eco-Hero Awards for the 9–13 age group for his fantastic work in protecting Atlantic horseshoe crabs near his home in Maryland, USA.

Alexander also founded Planet Horseshoe Crab, the flagship project at the Chesapeake Conservation Center in Maryland, USA.

Alexander Zerphy

Alexander designed the Planet Horseshoe Crab logo.

Horseshoe Crabs

The horseshoe crab is one of the oldest creatures on Earth, having been around for over 455 million years. Fossil remains show that it has not changed much in that time. Although horseshoe crabs have hard shells and claws like crabs, they are more closely related to spiders and scorpions. There are only four species of horseshoe crab. They are found along the South-East Asian and North-West Atlantic coasts and in the Gulf of Mexico.

Atlantic horseshoe crab

Atlantic horseshoe crabs in the surf

LIFE SCIENCE FEATURE

Atlantic Horseshoe Crabs

The Horseshoe Crab's Blood

The scientific name for the Atlantic horseshoe crab is *Limulus polyphemus.* Cells extracted from the blood of Atlantic horseshoe crabs are called "Limulus Amoebocyte Lysate" (LAL).

The LAL cells are used by scientists to test for the presence of harmful bacteria in blood, vaccines and prescription medication. LAL is also used to test if harmful bacteria is present on surgical instruments before they are used in operations.

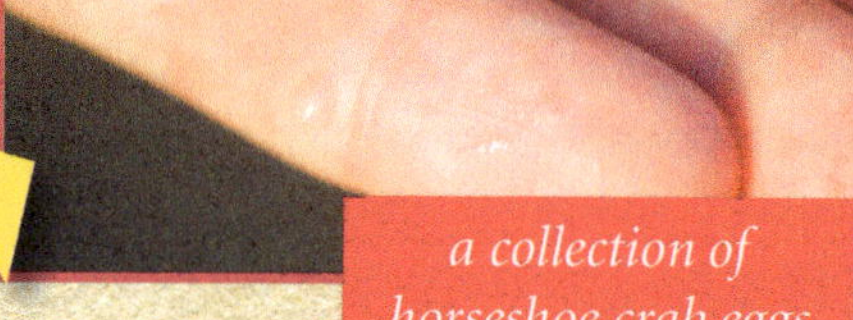

a collection of horseshoe crab eggs

How Alexander Got Started

Alexander started his project the day he discovered Atlantic horseshoe eggs in the sand at a nearby beach. To mark the spot where he first found the eggs, Alexander later put up a sign telling people to keep a watchful eye out for the Atlantic horseshoe crabs and their eggs.

Alexander Frees Horseshoe Crabs

When Alexander Zerphy sees a stranded horseshoe crab on its back, he immediately flips it over. Sometimes the horseshoe crabs get wedged between rock walls, so he frees them. An Atlantic horseshoe crab has gills under its body that enable it to breathe in or out of water, but if it can't get back to the water the gills dry out – and that's fatal!

Alex frees a wedged horseshoe crab.

THE HORSESHOE CRAB'S SHELL

Chitin is a protein that is found in the hard outer shell that covers the top of the Atlantic horseshoe crab. It has healing properties, so it is used to coat surgical sutures (stitches) and wound dressings for burn victims. Chitin is also used to help make contact lenses!

4 An Eco-Hero Procedure

TEXT TYPE
Procedure
PAGES 15–17

Goal

To become an eco-hero.

Essentials

You will need:

- a local habitat such as wetlands, bushland, forest, a beach or a park
- an endangered species belonging to that habitat
- a passion for nature
- time
- creativity

Alexander flips a horseshoe crab over so it can walk again.

see steps on pages 16 and 17

Steps

Step 1
Explore Nature

Go to the local habitat you have chosen. Look for signs indicating the presence of your chosen endangered species.

Alexander Zerphy discovered clear orbs with "alien-looking creatures swimming inside".

horseshoe crab orbs (eggs)

Step 2
Undertake Research

Undertake research on your chosen endangered species to find out its interesting characteristics and the threats to its survival.

Alexander found out that the orbs were the unhatched eggs of the Atlantic horseshoe crab. While it wasn't an endangered species, he discovered that habitat destruction by humans was a problem. He also discovered that its blue blood had a vital "ingredient" that helped doctors to detect harmful bacteria.

Step 3
Become Involved in Protecting Your Chosen Endangered Species

Participate in a project that aims to protect the endangered species you have chosen.

Alexander joined the Maryland Department of Natural Resources project to help protect the Atlantic horseshoe crab.

Step 4
Promote the Protection of Your Chosen Endangered Species

Create a campaign to promote the importance of protecting the endangered species you have chosen.

Alexander created a logo and then he wrote fact cards about the Atlantic horseshoe crab. His fact cards reminded people that they share the horseshoe crabs' beach ecosystem.

Step 5
Create a Conservation Program

Work with a team to create a conservation program that educates people about the importance to the environment of the endangered species you have chosen.

Alexander funded a conservation centre with his own money. He wrote more fact cards and organised T-shirts.

Step 6
Ask for Help

Talk to government representatives to discuss how they can help to protect your chosen endangered species.

Alexander spoke to the mayor of his city. The mayor arranged for two large information boards to be installed at the local maritime museum beach and at a nature park. Alexander's facts were featured on the boards.

Alexander holds a young horseshoe crab.

Step 7
Educate People

Write an educational program for use with students and adults.

Alexander was invited by a local maritime museum to teach Atlantic horseshoe crab ecology to students aged between five and 13 years old, and adults, too.

Alexander Today

Alexander continues to educate people about the Atlantic horseshoe crab and other local marine species. He is also the student adviser for the local Terrapin Institute, which works to protect coastal habitats and their inhabitants.

5 Rainforest Eco-Heroes

Many people around the world are rainforest eco-heroes. So why do so many people care about rainforests when they only cover about two per cent of Earth?

First of all, rainforests convert tonnes of carbon dioxide into clean air for us to breathe, via photosynthesis.

Secondly, the world's rainforests are the oldest living ecosystems on Earth and the home of:

millions of indigenous people

over half of all Earth's plant and animal species

many plants that people use to make medicines and other health products.

morning mist over dense tropical rainforest in Kaeng Krachan, Thailand

Earth's rainforests are home to an amazing array of flora and fauna.

Rainforests Rapidly Declining

For many years, companies have been logging rainforests, for timber and to clear space for mines, settlements and crops, such as coffee beans and sugar cane. Clearing rainforests threatens the homes of the local people. It also threatens thousands of plant and animal species, many of which live exclusively in rainforests.

Did You Know?

There are more fish species in the Amazon River system than in the Atlantic Ocean.

Amazon Indian women, in a rainforest in Ecuador

The Amazon Rainforest

The Amazon tropical rainforest is the largest rainforest in the world.

Did You Know?

About one third of Earth's bird species are found in the Amazon rainforest.

A Rainforest Eco-Hero Organisation

Around the world, there are many people and organisations working hard to prevent further destruction of rainforests. One rainforest eco-hero organisation is Rainforest Action Network (RAN), based in San Francisco, USA.

RAN's mission is to campaign for the rainforests, and for the indigenous peoples and the plant and animal species living in them. RAN's work involves educating people and organising non-violent action campaigns. RAN believes that things like logging ancient rainforests to supply photocopy paper, or destroying endangered ecosystems for oil, are unnecessary and not sustainable.

RAN hopes that by educating people, they can spread the message that today's technology enables us to recycle paper for photocopying purposes. We also have many alternative energy sources to oil. Using renewable energy sources helps to reduce our impact on the environment.

reflections on the Amazon River, Brazil

Social Studies

Indigenous Rainforest Communities

Millions of indigenous people live in rainforests. The Penan people, for example, live in the rainforests of Borneo. The Huli live in the mountain rainforests of Papua New Guinea. The Krikati live in the Amazon Rainforest in Brazil. For many centuries, these and other indigenous peoples have depended on rainforests for shelter, food and safety.

The Krikati are one of the indigenous peoples of Brazil. They inhabit a large territory in the Brazilian part of the Amazon Rainforest.

rainforest logging

6 Postie Eco-Heroes

GREEN

Australia Post makes millions of mail deliveries every year. Their post delivery staff, also called "posties", use motorcycles, vans and trucks to deliver mail to Australia's urban and rural areas.

Australia Post also has an employee called the Head of Sustainability. It's their job to come up with great ways to make delivering the mail more environmentally friendly.

Electrically Assisted Bicycles

In 2011, Australia Post became an eco-hero organisation when it supplied bicycles and tricycles, some pedal-powered and some electrically assisted, to 1000 posties! By replacing the motorcycles that those posties had been using, Australia Post reduced its yearly carbon dioxide emissions by about 1000 tonnes.

Australia Post is one of Australia's biggest employers, so this eco-action is a significant one for the environment.

an eco-hero postie

The Bike's **Specs!**

Speed

An electrically assisted bicycle can travel at speeds of up to 25 kilometres an hour. The posties can use "pedal power" on flat sections of road and then switch to electrical power on the hills.

Technology

Bike Batteries

The bike's lithium ion battery is made from lightweight materials. It lasts longer than the heavier lead acid batteries, because it can be charged a greater number of times.

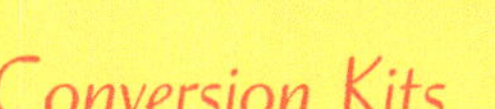

Conversion Kits

Most pedal-powered bicycles and tricycles can be upgraded. A specialist can turn a pedal-powered bike into an electrically assisted bike by fitting it with a conversion kit.

Distance

An electrically assisted bike's battery can provide power for up 40 kilometres.

Instead of listening for his motorcycle, people now listen for this postie's whistle.

7 Can Cars Be Eco-Heroes?

The car was first used as a passenger vehicle about 110 years ago. Today, there are over 600 million vehicles on the road. Most of those vehicles are petrol-powered and together they emit huge amounts of carbon dioxide into the atmosphere. Big vehicles like trucks, buses and four-wheel drives emit more pollution than smaller vehicles.

Every year, car manufacturers find new ways to design cars that use less fuel and emit less carbon dioxide into the air. One way to do this is to design cars with diesel-powered engines or electric motors, which have better fuel economy.

Hybrid cars are not a new idea as shown by this prototype on display at Expo 1974, in the USA.

a hybrid car being refuelled

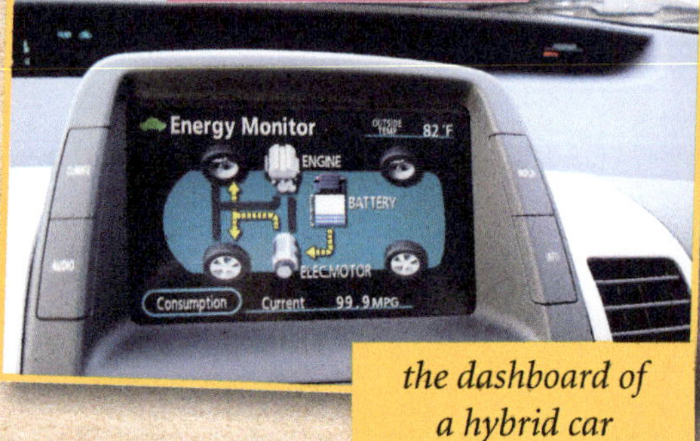

the dashboard of a hybrid car

In 2011, Australia had 16 million motor vehicles (mostly cars and motorbikes)

Canada 26 million

UK 31 million

USA 250 million

HOW MANY NEW VEHICLES?

In the USA and the UK, the number of motor vehicles being purchased has dropped for the first time in many years, but in Australia, the number of cars is increasing each year.

Hybrid Electric Cars

Most hybrid electric cars use both a petrol-powered (or gas-powered) engine and an electric motor. Some advantages of hybrid cars are:

- they have better fuel economy
- they don't emit as much carbon dioxide
- they're quieter than other types of vehicles.

One disadvantage is that they cost more money to buy than petrol or diesel vehicles because they are expensive to build.

The Peugeot hybrid sports car was raced in England, in 2008.

hybrid concept car

Am I an Eco-Hero Car?

Clues

- My small aerodynamic shape creates less drag, so I need less power which means less fuel.
- My shape and my electric motor mean that I use 5.6 litres of fuel to travel 100 kilometres, which is only half as much fuel as other medium-sized cars use.
- I have been described as cute and comfortable.
- My 1.2 litre engine is about half to a third of the size of my larger car cousins.
- I have many safety features, including airbags and electronic stability control.
- I am particularly fuel-efficient in city traffic where I have to stop and start many times.
- The Australian Government's *Green Vehicle Guide* gave me a five-star rating.

a hybrid car called the Lumeneo Smera, on display in Paris in 2010

8 Wanted: More Ocean Eco-Heroes

WANTED

Oceans cover 90 per cent of Earth. Many people are working hard to clear the oceans of pollution and to protect the world's largest marine ecosystem from activities that cause more pollution.

World Oceans Day, held on 8 June every year, is one way to draw everyone's attention to the importance of protecting the oceans. On World Oceans Day, people celebrate the millions of amazing marine animals in the oceans that rely on unpolluted water for survival. The celebrations also motivate people to plan eco-hero activities for the whole year.

clown fish hiding

World Ocean Network

World Oceans Day is jointly organised by the World Ocean Network (WON) and a United States association called The Ocean Project. WON is one of the many ocean eco-hero organisations that has created projects to:

1. protect endangered species
2. reduce marine pollution
3. encourage responsible activity.

a school of surgeonfish swimming around the Great Barrier Reef coral

Ocean Eco-Actions

Many responsible people work together to protect the millions of marine species that inhabit the world's oceans. Some areas of activity are described below.

Plastic Pollution: Cleaning up the millions of plastic items polluting the oceans so animals don't get tangled in or swallow them.

Reefs at Risk: Finding scientific evidence to help focus people's efforts. For example, in 2011, the World Resources Institute reported that about 75 per cent of the world's coral reefs are at risk, mainly due to irresponsible fishing practices. This evidence showed that the problem is worsening.

Untreated Waste Pollution: Working in coastal areas to prevent untreated waste and contaminated water from entering oceans from companies, farms and homes.

Marine Pollution: Lobbying for stricter laws to prevent waste entering the oceans from ships and sea-based oil and gas projects.

CORAL BLEACHING

Warmer ocean temperatures caused by global warming make corals lose their colour and die.

an example of coral bleaching

Rubbish litters a beach in Acapulco, Mexico, after a storm.

Food **Chain** Pollution

When oceans are polluted, marine food chains are affected – from the smallest organisms at the bottom to the predators at the top of the food chain.

Animals that consume contaminated food pass on the toxins or poisons to the next animal in the food chain.

Polar bears are especially at risk because toxins build up in fatty areas, and polar bears have a lot of fat to keep them warm.

An Arctic Food Chain

Algae

Shrimp

Arctic Cod

Polar Bear

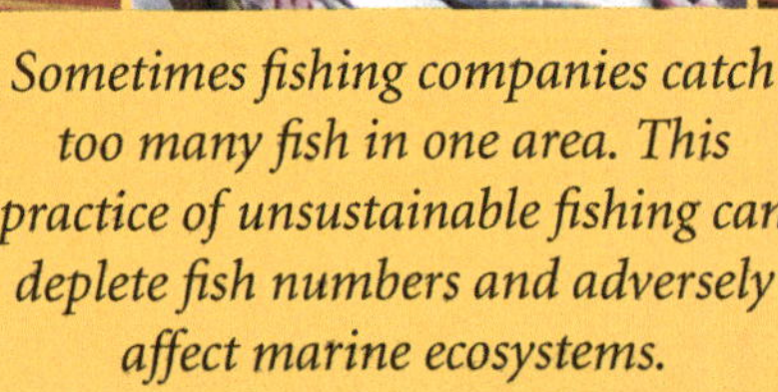

Sometimes fishing companies catch too many fish in one area. This practice of unsustainable fishing can deplete fish numbers and adversely affect marine ecosystems.

OCEAN ADVENTURER FEATURE

Roz Savage

Roz Savage

For many years, Roz Savage worked as a consultant in the UK. But like many people, she became very concerned about ocean pollution.

Roz wondered how one person could make a difference when there was so much plastic pollution in the oceans. Then she worked out a way: Roz decided to row across the oceans, oar stoke by oar stoke, so she could show people that every small action helps to achieve big goals.

In 2005, Roz Savage became an eco-hero when she began her rowing campaign. Since Roz began her solo rowing adventures, she has accomplished many goals.

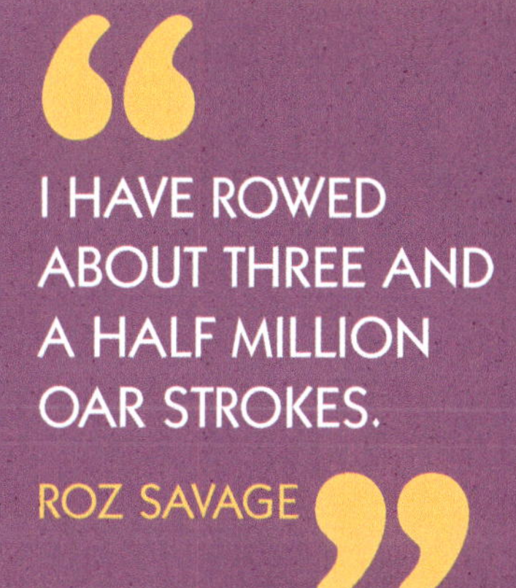

Ocean Campaigner

Roz has campaigned about pollution in our oceans. She writes articles on what she has seen during her ocean travels and talks about her experiences to the media.

A Rowing First

In 2010, Roz became the first woman to row solo across the Pacific Ocean. Roz is a brave adventurer who has rowed almost 18 000 kilometres to remind people about the need to clean up and protect Earth's biggest ecosystem.

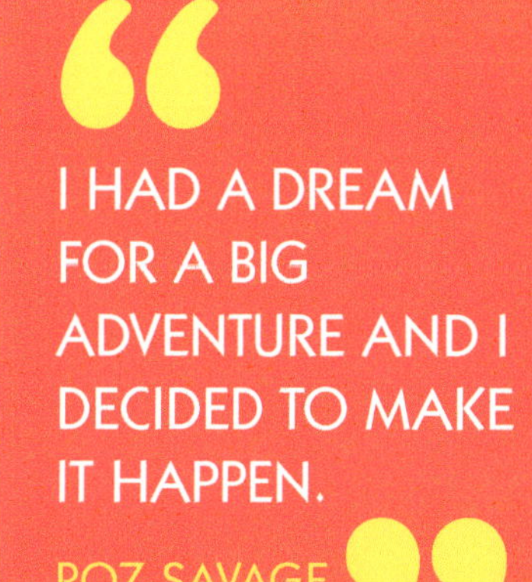

9 Stormwater Eco-Heroes

Stormwater run-off usually contains pollutants, which run into our waterways. The run-off can also cause soil erosion.

BIOFILTRATION

"Biofiltration" is when natural materials and vegetation are used to capture and remove pollutants and solid particles from stormwater.

Recycling Stormwater

An Australian engineering company called Biofilta has developed a new biofiltration system to capture and recycle stormwater run-off for use in parks. The new system will divert stormwater run-off from drains to an underground tank. There, the stormwater will be treated and stored as clean water for use in local parks as required.

The biofiltration system uses natural filters, such as triple-washed sand and native plants.

Science

Stormwater Pollutants

Stormwater gathers pollutants from roofs, gutters, roads and drains before it flows into waterways. One of the most common pollutants in stormwater is detergent from people washing their cars.

Biofilta's architectural drawings show the rain garden that forms part of the stormwater recycling project in the City of Melbourne.

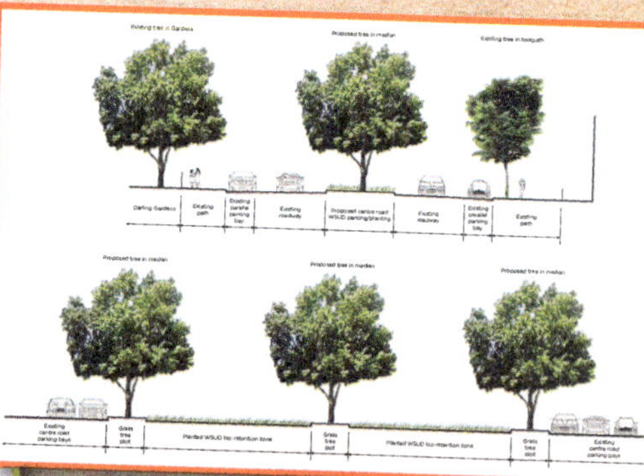

Biofilta's architectural drawings show another perspective, or view, of the stormwater recycling project.

Natural Environment: in areas covered in plants, only about 15 per cent of the rain that falls runs off as stormwater.

a natural environment

Built Environment: in a city or town with more buildings, concrete paths and roads, about 85 per cent of the rainfall runs off into waterways.

a built-up environment

The City of Melbourne's inner areas are built up.

I'm a water-saving eco-hero. See me on page 6.

Survey Reveals Top 100 Eco-Heroes

In the United Kingdom (UK), the Environment Agency decided to ask environmental experts to name the top 100 eco-heroes who have done the most work to save the planet. The 2006 survey honoured Father Christmas with place number 100 for his carbon-free delivery of presents worldwide!

Index

Glossary

contaminated Unclean or unsafe because waste or chemicals have got mixed in

drag The force that slows down a vehicle due to air resistance

ecosystem A network of plants and animals all depending on each other in their natural environment

endangered species A species that is threatened in its natural habitat, and faces a serious danger of becoming extinct

habitat The environment in which a plant or animal lives naturally

orb A rounded shape, or sphere

sustainable Able to be continued without hurting the environment or running out of natural resources

stormwater The water that runs off into gutters and waterways when it rains heavily, rather than being absorbed into the ground

terrapin Any of several kinds of North American turtle